Rain Forests

Joy Palmer

RSVP

RAINTREE
STECK-VAUGHN
P U B L I S H E R S
The Steck-Vaughn Company
Austin, Texas

Editor: Ambreen Husain
Designer: Shaun Barlow
Project Manager: Joyce Spicer
Electronic Production: Scott Melcer
Artwork: Hayward Art Group
Cover Art: Hayward Art Group

Educational Advisor:
   Joy Richardson
Consultant: Miranda MacQuitty

Library of Congress
Cataloging-in-Publication Data
Palmer, Joy.
     Rain forests / Joy Palmer.
         p.   cm. — (What About)
     Includes index.
     Summary: Describes the plants, animals, and human inhabitants of a tropical rain forest and discusses the importance of these unique environments and threats to their survival.
     Hardcover   ISBN 0-8114-3400-1
     Softcover   ISBN 0-8114-4911-4
     1. Rain forests — Juvenile literature. 2. Rain forest ecology—Juvenile literature. 3. Rain forest conservation—Juvenile literature. [1. Rain forests. 2. Rain forest ecology. 3. Ecology.]   I. Title.
II. Series.
QH86.P35 1992
574.5'2642'0913—dc20   92-10634
                                            CIP
                                            AC
Printed and bound in the United States by Lake Book, Melrose Park, IL

     7 8 9 0 LB 00 99 98 97

Contents

What Are Rain Forests?

Rain forests are made up of tall trees and many other plants, all growing closely together. They cover huge areas of land. It is always hot and damp inside a rain forest, so plants keep growing all year round. Rain forests are home to the greatest variety of plants and animals in the world. People live there, too.

▽ The Amazon rain forest is the largest in the world.

Where Are Rain Forests?

Most rain forests grow in hot, wet parts of the world called the **tropics**. The tropics are near the **equator**. The equator is an imaginary line around the middle of the Earth, where the weather is warmest. Tropical rain forests are only found in countries near the equator.

Do you live in a tropical area?

▷ This rain forest is on a tropical island.

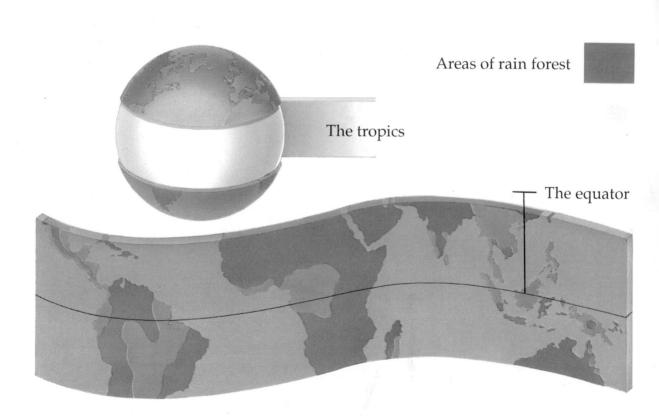

Areas of rain forest

The tropics

The equator

What Are Rain Forests Like?

It is hot and dark, and often wet, inside a rain forest. Many forest trees are very tall and grow close together. Their leaves and branches act like an umbrella, blocking out the strong sunlight. This thick top layer of leaves and branches is called the forest **canopy**. Shorter trees and other plants grow under the canopy between the taller trees.

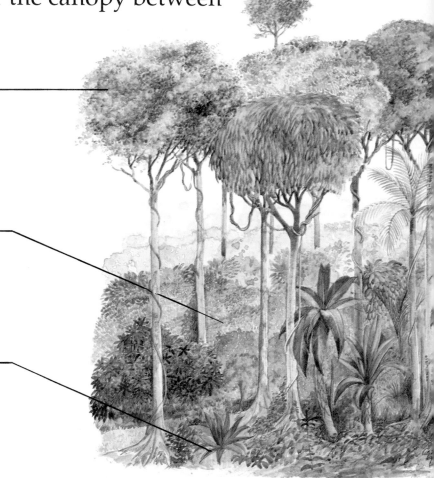

Canopy

The canopy is the top layer of the forest. It gets almost all the sunlight and rainfall.

Understory

The understory is a place of shade. Very little sunlight reaches the plants that grow there.

Forest floor

Very little grows on the dark forest floor. It is always covered with fallen leaves, flowers, and twigs.

Emergents

A few very tall trees stand out high above the canopy. They are called emergents.

What Is the Weather Like?

Rain forests are hot and wet all year round. The trees help to make the rain. Big roots soak up water from the ground. The water is sucked up through the trunk into the leaves. The heat makes the water in the leaves **evaporate** into the air. This **water vapor condenses** to make clouds. Rain clouds release the rain onto the forest again.

▷ The air inside a rain forest feels warm and damp.

▽ There are often heavy rainstorms, which leave forest plants dripping with water.

Plants

Trees are the largest rain forest plants. Many rain forest trees have huge roots that show above the ground. These are called **buttress roots**. Many other plants grow underneath the trees. Some plants hang like thick ropes around the trunks and branches. Others live on the bark of the tree trunks. Many rare and unusual flowering plants grow in rain forests.

▷ The climbing pepper vine grows over other plants in sunlit clearings.

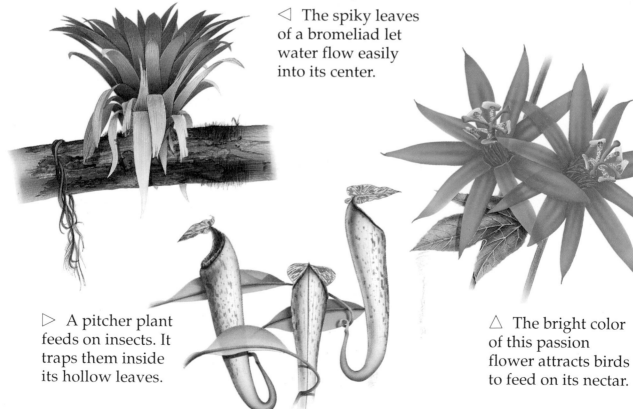

◁ The spiky leaves of a bromeliad let water flow easily into its center.

▷ A pitcher plant feeds on insects. It traps them inside its hollow leaves.

△ The bright color of this passion flower attracts birds to feed on its nectar.

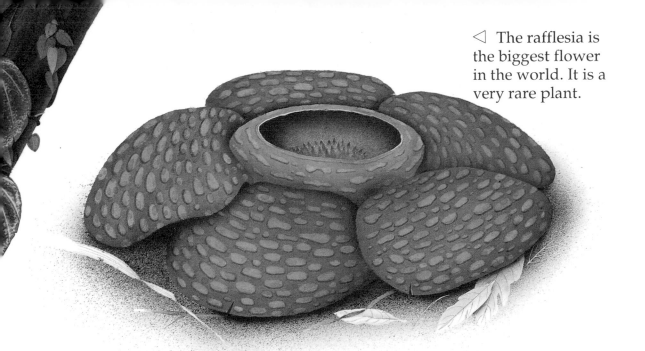

◁ The rafflesia is the biggest flower in the world. It is a very rare plant.

▽ Buttress roots help support the great weight of these trees.

11

Animals

Animals live at every level of the forest. Some live in the light, leafy treetops where they find food and shelter. Monkeys swing through the canopy. Snakes slither along branches in search of frogs and birds. Jaguars climb up trees to sit on low branches. Some animals stay on the ground, hunting for food near riverbanks and among low plants.

△ The sloth has long claws. They help it to cling to tree trunks and branches.

▷ The fruit bat sucks the juice from fruits and drops the seeds. It helps to spread the seeds.

▽ The jaguar has a spotted coat. This helps it to hide among the trees when it hunts.

▽ The anaconda is one of the world's largest snakes. It lives in or near water.

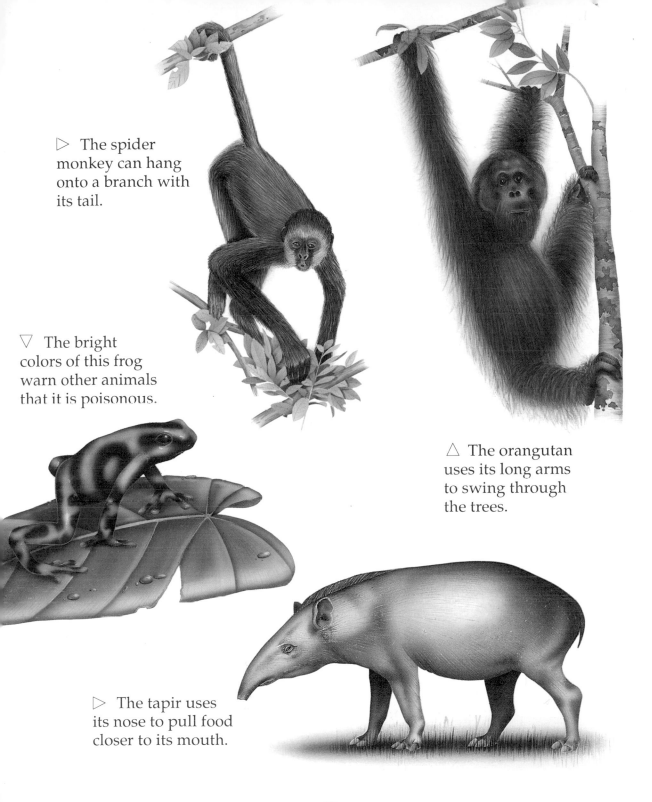

▷ The spider monkey can hang onto a branch with its tail.

▽ The bright colors of this frog warn other animals that it is poisonous.

△ The orangutan uses its long arms to swing through the trees.

▷ The tapir uses its nose to pull food closer to its mouth.

Birds

Brightly colored birds, like the macaw, nest in the trees. They fly from branch to branch in search of food. Some birds are fruit eaters, and some birds are seed eaters. Many smaller birds feed on insects or **nectar**. Some birds, like the nightjar, live on the ground. They peck for food on the forest floor.

△ The hummingbird's long, thin beak can reach the nectar inside flowers.

▽ The dark colors of the nightjar help it to hide on the forest floor.

▷ The toucan feeds mainly on fruit. It helps spread the fruit trees' seeds.

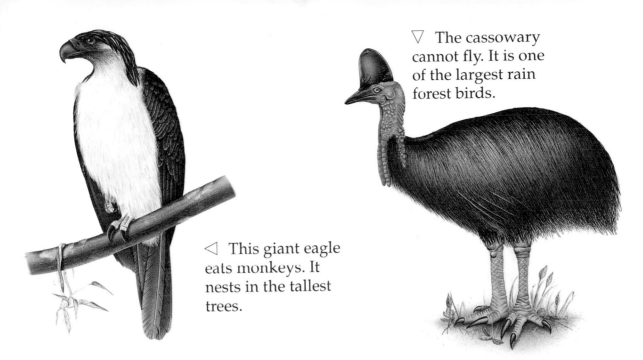

▽ The cassowary cannot fly. It is one of the largest rain forest birds.

◁ This giant eagle eats monkeys. It nests in the tallest trees.

▽ Macaws can use their hard beaks to scratch rocks for salt.

Insects and Spiders

Millions of tiny creatures such as insects and spiders live on the trees and in the undergrowth. Beetles, ants, and termites crawl among the dead leaves on the forest floor. They help to break up this **forest litter**. Butterflies and moths fly between the flowering plants, searching for nectar. They help to spread pollen from flower to flower.

▷ Leaf-cutter ants take leaves to their nests. They use them to make food.

▽ Termites help to clean the forest floor. They feed on dead wood.

▷ This blue morpho butterfly has brown underwings to help it hide among leaves.

◁ The bright colors of this shield bug warn attackers that it is poisonous.

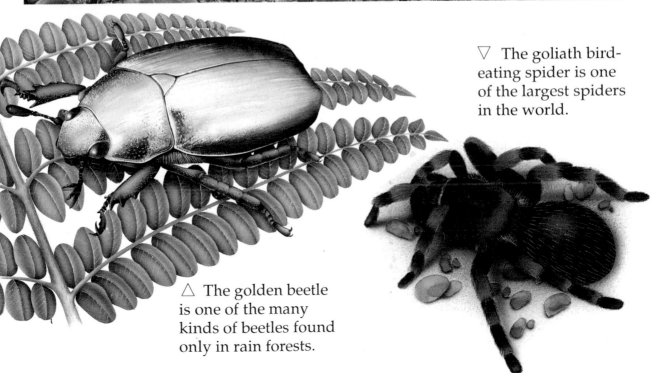

△ The golden beetle is one of the many kinds of beetles found only in rain forests.

▽ The goliath bird-eating spider is one of the largest spiders in the world.

People

People have lived in tropical rain forests for thousands of years. The forest provides them with food, shelter, clothes, tools, and medicines. Today there are millions of people living in rain forests around the world. They belong to different groups or **tribes**, each with its own customs.

▷ Many forest tribes live in a village in a space cleared of trees.

▽ The Kayapo hunt and grow crops in the forests of Brazil.

△ The Baka Pygmies live in the rain forests of West Africa.

△ The Uru Eu Wau Wau, like many rain forest people, paint their bodies.

How the People Live

Rain forest people hunt animals for meat to eat. They also gather berries, fruits, and the roots of some plants.

Some tribes clear away trees to make a small space for growing food crops. This is called slash-and-burn farming. The space is farmed for a few years. Then the people move on to a new place. The forest grows back on the land they leave.

▽ Hunters also use bows and arrows to reach animals high in the canopy.

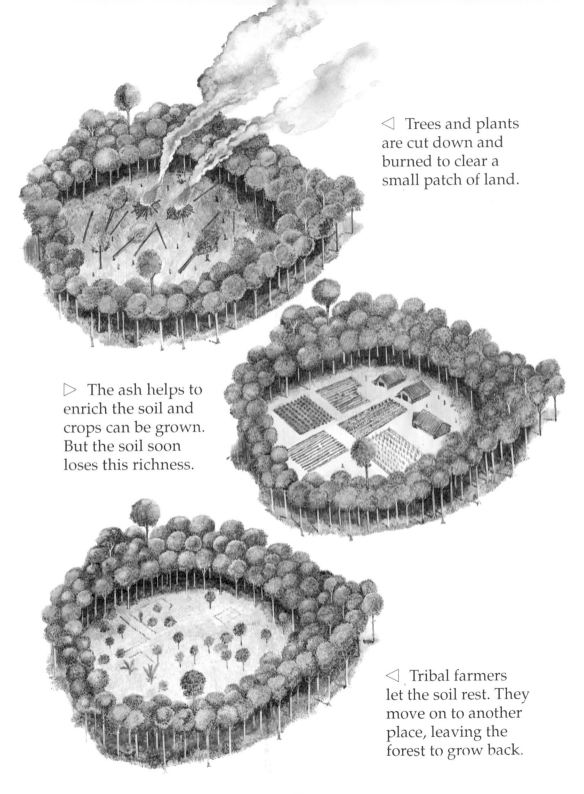

◁ Trees and plants are cut down and burned to clear a small patch of land.

▷ The ash helps to enrich the soil and crops can be grown. But the soil soon loses this richness.

◁ Tribal farmers let the soil rest. They move on to another place, leaving the forest to grow back.

Surviving in the Rain Forest

Rain forest people know how to get everything they need from the forest without destroying the trees forever. They know how to prepare roots for eating, and how parts of some plants can be used as medicines. They know which berries are not poisonous and where to find sweet honey in the forest.

▷ Rain forest people get honeycombs from honeybee nests high in the canopy.

▽ Rain forest plants are used to make everyday items such as rope and baskets.

Why We Need Rain Forests

Many of the things we use every day come from rain forests. Rain forest plants are important for another reason. All plants take in **carbon dioxide**. Carbon dioxide is in the air we breathe. When too many trees are cut down, more carbon dioxide stays in the air. Carbon dioxide traps heat, so the air around the Earth gets warmer. This can cause serious problems for the Earth.

▽ Many of our medicines come from rain forest plants.

▽ Rattan furniture is made from rain forest plants.

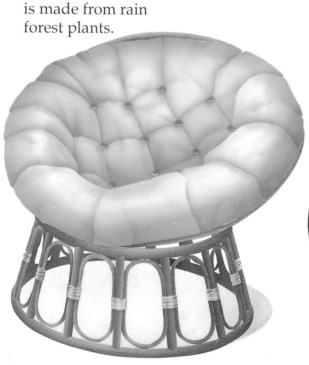

▷ Rain forest rubber is used to make many useful things.

◁ Pineapples and guavas are some of the fruits that grow in rain forests.

▷ Chewing gum is made using chicle from sapodilla trees.

▽ Rubber is made from latex collected from rubber trees.

Threats to the Rain Forest

Thousands of rain forest trees are being cut down or burned to make space for farmland, roads, buildings, or **mines**. Every second an area of forest twice the size of a football field is destroyed. When trees are removed, rain washes away the soil. Serious floods may occur. Many different plants and animals are losing their homes and becoming **extinct**.

▷ Many trees were destroyed to make this landing strip for airplanes.

▷ Some land is cleared completely for mining minerals such as copper.

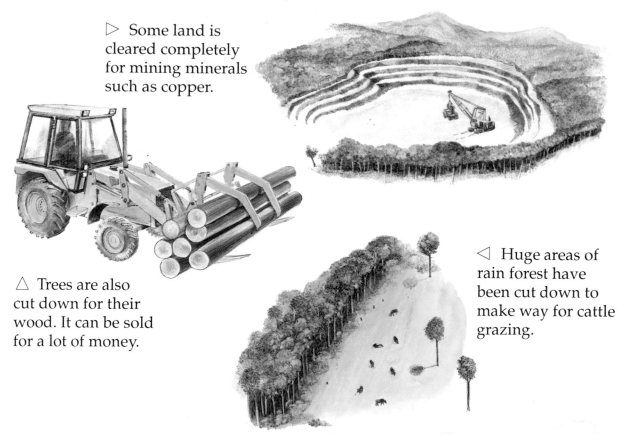

△ Trees are also cut down for their wood. It can be sold for a lot of money.

◁ Huge areas of rain forest have been cut down to make way for cattle grazing.

26

Saving the Rain Forests

There are many **conservation** groups working to save the world's rain forests. New trees are being planted to replace those that have been destroyed. In some countries there are areas of rain forest which are protected. These **forest preserves** also protect the wildlife. Much more could still be done. Everyone can help.

▷ Many different kinds of trees are being planted to help rain forest conservation.

▽ Many rain forest people are making their own protests against rain forest destruction.

Things to Do

- Make a poster to tell people about the importance of rain forests. Put it in your window or in your classroom.

- Visit your nearest botanical garden and enter the tropical house. It is hot and damp inside, like a rain forest.

- Grow your own rain forest plant at home. Plant an avocado pit in compost. Keep it in a light place and water it regularly.

Useful Addresses:

Conservation Foundation
1250 24th Street, N.W., Suite 500
Washington, DC 20037

Friends of the Earth
1045 Sansome Street
San Francisco, CA 94111

The Environmental Defense Fund
257 Park Avenue South, Dept. P
New York, NY 10010

Greenpeace
1611 Connecticut Avenue, N.W.
Washington, DC 20009

Glossary

buttress roots   Huge roots that develop to support heavy tree trunks and help keep very tall trees upright.

canopy   The top layer of leaves and branches in a rain forest.

carbon dioxide   A gas that is present in air. Air is made up of a mixture of gases, including oxygen and carbon dioxide. When we breathe, our bodies take in oxygen and give out carbon dioxide.

condenses   Changes from a gas into a liquid. Clouds are formed when water vapor condenses into very tiny droplets of water.

conservation   The protection of plants and animals and their natural homes, and the care of the land.

equator   The equator is an imaginary line around the middle of the Earth.

evaporate   Change from a liquid into a gas.

extinct   When every member of a type of animal or plant dies, it is said to be extinct. It is gone forever.

forest litter   A layer of dead leaves, twigs, and flowers on the forest floor.

forest preserve   An area of forest set apart for the protection of wildlife and nature.

mines   Places from which minerals are dug out of the ground. Copper and gold are minerals.

nectar   A sweet liquid produced by the flowers of many plants. It is food for insects and some birds.

tribes   Groups of people who share the same social customs and beliefs and live together in the same area.

tropics   The tropics are areas near the equator, on either side of it.

water vapor   Water in the form of a gas or a very fine mist.

31

Index

Photographic credits: Bruce Coleman Ltd. (G. Cubitt) 11, (G. Ziesler) cover, 15, (L. C. Marigo) 29; Ecoscene (D. Pearson) 25; Environmental Picture Library (S. Cunningham) 27; Susan Griggs Agency (V. Englebert) 20; OSF (G. I. Bernard) 5, (J. A. L. Cooke) 17; South American Pictures (T. Morrison) cover, 3, 19, (B. Leimbach) 23; Zefa (H. Steenmans) 5.